T0114239

Treasures In The Valley

By

Sarah J. Blevins

First published by AuthorHouse 04/29/04

ISBN: 1-4184-5916-X (e-book)
ISBN: 1-4184-4928-8 (Paperback)

Printed in the United States of America
Bloomington, Indiana

This book is printed on acid free paper.

Credit For Graphics: US Fish and Wildlife Service

Scripture taken from the Amplified Bible,
Old Testament copyright © 1965, 1987 by
The Zandervan Corporation. The Amplified
New Testament copyright © 1958, 1987 by The
Lockman Foundation. Used by permission.

HIS BLESSINGS ARE FLOWING OVER ME

His blessings are flowing over me like a river of grace from above.
I didn't know my Father's heart was filled with so much love.

I am His beloved daughter-an alien no more.
I'm not wandering through the desert as I was before.

From a blinded child to someone who can see,
From a pauper to a princess-that's what Jesus did for me.

The waters of confusion rose far above my head.
But there He was reaching out to give me life instead.

His blessings are flowing over me like a river of grace from above.
I didn't know my Father's heart was filled with so much love.

Now, His joy is my desire-I want to bless Him in return.
The fire He filled my heart with will never cease to burn.

His Holy Spirit comforts me as He holds me in His arms,
Safe from anything that would try to bring me harm

A WILTED ROSE

God can take a wilted rose and turn it into a beautiful flower.
He can change the desert land by flooding it with a shower.

He has a Father's heart that beats for you and me.
His love is never ending. It flows warm and free.

A world that's built on sand will one day surely fall,
but God is still there listening, just waiting for our call.

God can take a wilted rose and turn it into a beautiful flower.
He can change the desert land by flooding it with a shower.

In the hardest times of life, good things can come to be,
because God can work in weakness and He can set the prisoner free.

A world that's built on sand will one day surely fall,
but God is still there listening, just waiting for our call.

God can take a wilted rose and turn it into a beautiful flower.
He can change the desert land by flooding it with a shower.

He has a Father's heart that beats for you and me.
His love is never ending. It flows warm and free.

IF I COULD

I would take all of your pain and struggles if I could
but then you would be like a butterfly-unable to fly if I would.

I might turn every mountain into a hill, making it easier to climb
or uncover every treasure so it is easy to find.

Every storm that might pass over, I could send it another way
but if everything were that easy, would you find the time to pray?

My pearls don't become jewels just by fleeting chance.
It takes a lot of struggle for a dancer to learn to dance.

My heart's desire is to never see you in pain
but the vanity of this world would cause you to live in vain.

As a mother who grieves when her child falls down
so, my heart hurts too, when my children stumble to the ground.

In my love, sometimes I must let you learn through pain
but unlike the vanity of this world it will not be in vain.

Still, I remain merciful and full of love for you
and every trial that you must face-I will bring you through.

I remember hearing a story about a young boy who decided to try and help a caterpillar out of its cocoon. The intentions were good, however the butterfly's wings ended up being crippled and ultimately it died. It needed the struggle of coming out of the cocoon to gain strength. So many times I have asked God for things. I thought it was just a matter of asking then receiving. Sometimes, that was the case, but other times I really had to struggle. What I learned was that in the struggle I grew immensely. In His love for me there are times He has to allow it.

Consider it wholly joyful my brethren, whenever you are enveloped in or encounter trials of any sort or fall into various temptations. Be assured and understand that the trial and the proving of your faith bring out endurance and steadfastness and patience.

James 1:2-3

HOLY SPIRIT

Here I am, Here I am, listening for your voice;
Here I am waiting, Lord, then I will rejoice.

I never found a friend so true, I never knew such love;
I find you here right next to me, not just far above.

The sounds I hear from busyness now get in the way,
so here I am in quietness, listening to what you say.

I know that you're not satisfied with just a part of me.
Teach me to surrender and teach me how to be.

Here I am, Here I am, listening for your voice;
Here I am waiting, Lord, then I will rejoice.

I hear the sweetness of your words, I will not turn away.
I'll come with you to the mountaintop and find you when I pray.

I never found a friend so true, I never knew such love;
I find you here right next to me, not just far above.

Holy Spirit you are my comforter, with me for ever more;
I will not run away from you, just unlock all the doors.

Here I am, here I am, listening for your voice.
Here I am waiting, Lord, then I will rejoice.

For the promise (of the Holy Spirit) is to and for you and your
children, and to and for all that are far away, (even) to and for as
many as the Lord our God invites and bids to come to Himself.

Acts 2:39

I BELIEVE IN YOU

I was searching all my life for the perfect friend.
I wanted to trust in their love and believe it wouldn't end.

I looked in the eyes of strangers hoping they would be the one
but all I saw were searching eyes looking too for love.

Out of nowhere it seems you came looking just for me.
Jesus, I believe in you-you let my heart go free.

I prayed for strength so I may stand, but you gave me wings to fly.
How could it be you chose to love someone such as I?

Your grace you gave immeasurably, your mercy knew no end.
You're the one I was searching for-you are the perfect friend.

Out of nowhere it seems you came looking just for me.
Jesus, I believe in you-you let my heart go free.

I prayed for strength so I may stand, but you gave me wings to fly.
How could it be you chose to love someone such as I?

*The Lord appeared from of old to me (Israel), saying, Yes, I have
loved you with an everlasting love; therefore with loving-kindness
have I drawn you and continued My faithfulness to you.*

Jeremiah 31:3

BEHOLD HIS GLORY

Behold the glory of the Lord in the rushing of the sea,
or the way the eagle flies unhindered and free.

Behold the glory of the Lord in the storm that sweeps the land.
He is magnified by the thunder, the lightning — the works of His
hands.

See the mercy of the King with the scars in His side,
forgiving all who come to Him — His arms are open wide.

His splendor is revealed in the coming of the spring,
and heard in every note that the songbirds sing.

No other artist can create all the things He's done.
He's painted evening skies with the setting of the sun.

Behold His magnificent glory in all things great and small.
Give Him praise and honor, for He has created them all.

How lovely are your tabernacles, O Lord of Hosts!
My soul yearns, yes even pines and is homesick for the courts of
the Lord; my heart and my flesh cry out and sing for joy to the
living God.

Psalm 84:1-2

I WANT TO SEE YOU LORD

I want to see you in the morning, Lord, the first one that I see.
I want to look into your eyes as you gaze upon me.

Will you fill my days with many thoughts of you,
and bring me to the place where everything is new?

Let me bring glory to your name, Lord, let your love change all of me.
Look into my heart and teach me to be free.

I want to see you in the nighttime when I rest upon my bed.
Will you fill my heart with you and things that you have said?

When I wander in the meadow or lie beneath a tree,
I want to know I'm not alone, but you are resting there with me.

Let me bring glory to your name, Lord, let your love change all of me.
Look into my heart and teach me to be free.

I want to be in love with you and never change my mind.
I know there is no other love, I leave the rest behind.

Help me to be your child, growing to be like you
and help me overcome the things I don't want to do.

Let me bring glory to your name, Lord, let your love change all of me.
Look into my heart and teach me to be free.

I WILL WORSHIP YOU IN THE VALLEY

I will worship you in the valley where the flowers refuse to grow,
in the barren wilderness where the courageous don't want to go.

Let the praise from my lips rise far above the earth.
Let my voice declare the truth of your priceless worth.

I've known you in the hard place where sorrow would not cease
and I've known you in the restful place where my heart was filled with peace.

You have been my strong tower—a proven, faithful friend,
a canopy in the wilderness and a defense against the wind.

I will worship you in the valley where the flowers refuse to grow,
in the barren wilderness where the courageous don't want to go.

Let the praise from my lips rise far above the earth,
let my voice declare the truth of your priceless worth.

I want my life to be a song that I sing just for you.
I want to reflect your love in all I say or do.

Even though I struggle, your mighty hand is strong.
I will sing to you in worship—that's where my heart belongs.

I think it is relatively easy to worship God when things are going well. It's when they aren't that the real test comes. I love to praise the Lord. When all is well with me, it seems as if my heart is really in it. When things are tough, however, that's when it's even more important to praise. I used to think if my feelings didn't line up, then I wasn't obeying Him in this area. What I've learned is I am free from the whims of my emotions. I can still praise Him when I am down, or things aren't going so well.

Lord, I want to worship you in the valley just as fervently as I do on the mountaintop.

Praise the Lord, all you nations! Praise Him, all you people! For His mercy and loving-kindness are great toward us, and the truth and faithfulness of the Lord endure forever. Praise the Lord! (Hallelujah!)

Psalm 117

TREASURES IN THE VALLEY

There are treasures in the valley, this I've come to see.
There are jewels formed from the fire I thought afflicted me.

Passing through the darkness, I learned that I must rest
in His faithful promise no matter what the test.

God's strength is abundant, His arms embrace this child,
even in the valley He tempers every trial.

Jesus is the bridge over water that is too deep.
He is the one who carries me up hills that are too steep.

He's given pearls of wisdom and golden truths to me,
treasures in the valley, this I've come to see.

Passing through the darkness, I learned that I must rest
in His faithful promise no matter what the test.

The storms in life don't frighten me the way they used to do,
because I trust my Father to safely bring me through.

There are treasures in the valley, this I've come to see.
There are jewels formed from the fire I thought afflicted me.

Passing through the darkness I learned that I must rest
in His faithful promise no matter what the test.

Jesus is the bridge over water that is too deep.
He is the one who carries me up hills that are too steep.

BENEATH THE TARNISH LIES THE GOLD

If you wipe away the tarnish the gold is what you'll see.
In a heart born again, Jesus has the key.

If you look beyond the clouds and know they'll always pass,
you'll see hope that never dies and love that always lasts.

It is a sure foundation, the one built in Christ.
It's a refuge from the world, a place to start your life.

Your soul can only die if you choose to let that be,
but God says turn away from death, and He will set you free.

If you wipe away the tarnish the gold is what you'll see.
In a heart born again, Jesus has the key.

Who can make you stumble, or who can make you fall?
If your fortress is the Lord Himself, you possess it all.

It's not wealth within the world, it's life for eternity,
if you turn away from death, God will set you free.

It is a sure foundation, the one built in Christ.
It's a refuge from the world, a place to start your life.

If you wipe away the tarnish, the gold is what you'll see,
In a heart born again, Jesus has the key.

It's pretty cut and dry. If you have Jesus, you have life; if you don't, you have death. The only foundation that will stand forever is the one built in Christ. When I came to Jesus my heart was broken, my mind was broken, and I was in really bad shape. I didn't even know if there was hope for me. After struggling with mental illness for years, I was just hanging on. I became a Christian because I was doing things in my life that I knew were wrong. I had heard about Jesus through a friend of mine. I knew I was on the wrong side of the fence. My heart was convicted every day that the way I was living was wrong. What I didn't realize was that Jesus not only wanted to give me eternal life, He wanted to give me a good life here on earth, too. For the first time in years I had hope. My future wasn't to be mentally ill, but to be free in the freedom that He would give me.

I DIDN'T CHOOSE A MOUNTAIN TO CLIMB

I didn't choose a mountain to climb, I didn't choose the valley of weeping.
I didn't choose to suffer at all, but you told me to go on seeking.

First, it was your message about your glorious salvation.
Though I turned you down, you just kept on waiting.

You sent a friend who helped me see
accepting your Son as Savior was how that it must be.

Still, I didn't choose a mountain to climb, I didn't choose to go through the valley of weeping.
I didn't choose to suffer at all, but you told me to go on seeking.

Next, were the struggled attempts to reach your throne in prayer,
and I tried to find a formula, but it seemed you weren't there.

Sometimes it was so painful, but you just led the way.
Through struggled attempts and letting go, I've gone from night to day.

I've handed over dreams of mine, Lord, I give them all to you
trusting you know what's best for me, you'll show me what to do.

I didn't choose a mountain to climb, I didn't choose the valley of weeping.
I didn't choose to suffer at all, but you told me to go on seeking.

The valley of weeping for me was a battle with mental illness that began when I was a young teenager. I spent time in and out of hospitals with little hope. I couldn't find help in the hospitals or psychiatrists or my own intellectual reasoning, but I found hope and healing in Jesus. He said "by His stripes we are healed". Whether it be mental illness, cancer, diabetes, it doesn't matter. His promise is sure. We do the trusting and He does the healing. It didn't happen overnight, but it did happen. He brought me out of that valley and now "mental illness" for me, is a thing of the past. I thank Him for the mind He has given me, and I thank Him for taking me through the valley of weeping, because that is where I had to learn to lean on Him. The irony was that is what I needed to do all along. Not just because I had a crippling illness, but because no matter what, I can't or anyone can't really make it on their own. We are created for Him and any life outside of Him is a cheap imitation of the real thing. He is my Abba (daddy).

I NEED YOUR TENDERNESS

I feel like I've been a fighter in the middle of the ring.
I had to learn to fight when I wanted to sing.

I was only running away, while trying to be strong,
In the middle of the ring everything seemed wrong.

Jesus, I need your tenderness, the touches have been so few,
only you can touch my heart and take away the bruise.

I am not a fighter, I don't want to play that game.
I only need your tenderness to wash away the blame.

I took the blows of angry words, I became like steel,
but you can change a hardened heart—you long so much to heal.

Jesus, I need your tenderness, the touches have been so few,
only you can touch my heart and take away the bruise.

I feel like I've been a fighter in the middle of the ring.
I had to fight when I wanted to sing.

Jesus, I need your tenderness, the touches have been so few,
only you can touch my heart and take away the bruise.

For most of my childhood and early adult life, I fought my way through life. It seemed that anything that I wanted to achieve or do was a struggle. In my human strength I was determined not to let that be a deterrent. If the mountain that was in front of me was 10,000 miles high, I felt that I would find a way to climb it. I became very good at being strong-willed. After I gave my heart to Jesus, I turned from the typical rebellion, but being strong willed was another matter. It seemed that it was okay if I was doing "good, productive" things. There are so many things that I want to do. I have dreams that I want to accomplish. I approached achieving them in the same way I approached achieving anything in my life-sheer determination. Working hard has not been a problem. Giving up-well that is a totally different matter. I feel sometimes that it would be easier to move Mount Everest with a spoon than to just give up and wait on God. The emotions that I have encountered while I am in a position that I *must do that* are incredible. I have experienced emotions that I haven't felt since I was a little girl in a situation where I was powerless. God says wait- I say how long? I wouldn't mind waiting if He only told me how long. That, however would only defeat His purpose. I am sure He is trying to teach me to trust Him when I can't do anything. God says I don't have to fight my way through life. He wants to bring me into a Father-daughter relationship with Him-from slavery to sonship. The bruises are painful. That is why I was in the ring in the first place. I was running from the pain. Jesus is healing that pain. My job is to be still.

"Father, I need your grace and strength to give in".

IF THERE HAS TO BE A VALLEY, THERE MUST BE A SAVIOUR, TOO

I went for a walk in the meadow with flowers everywhere.
It seemed like the birds were a symphony with every player there.

The day was almost perfect and there was nothing on my mind,
but I didn't know around the bend just what I would find.

I knew there was a valley that was deep and dark and long,
but I thought I would walk around it, as I heard the birds in song.

Suddenly, I was there where I didn't want to go,
and my strength would never save me, I had sunk so low.

In the valley there was no singing, but the darkness made a sound.
It was a sound of fear and hopelessness and danger all around.

But, if there has to be a valley than there must be a Savior too.
It was there that I met Jesus, and he brought me safely through

I didn't choose the road that would take me to that place,
but only in the valley could I meet Him face to face.

IM GLAD FOR NEW BEGINNINGS

I'm glad for new beginnings; like sunshine after rain.
I'm glad for hope that lives and joy that comes again.

I'm thankful for the springtime rain that helps the blossoms grow,
and wakens all the new life beneath the winter snow.

My heart is satisfied with all the good I see,
I know that God has displayed is as a gift for me.

Life used to be so dreary, because I chose to see the bad.
I didn't know how to give thanks for the good things that I had.

I had to learn that life is good, regardless of my pain.
I chose to thank and praise God so it wouldn't be in vain.

He chose my body for His temple and my voice to sing His song,
in my weakest moments I learned how to be strong.

I'm glad for new beginnings; like sunshine after rain.
I'm glad for hope that lives and joy that comes again.

I'm thankful for the springtime rain that helps the blossoms grow
and wakens all the new life beneath the winter snow.

IN MY OWN TIME

In my own time things will change before your eyes,
the mountains, the rivers, the seas and the stars that fill the sky.

In my own time-that's the way that things must be,
the way I bring the rain, the way I part the sea.

Lord, I bow down before you, I give my life to you,
I want my heart to be your throne in everything I do.

By my love I made a way for my people to enter in,
by my love I gave my son, He has conquered sin.

I'm still waiting every day for ones who will bow down.
I am the Lord who created you, I made the world go round.

Lord I bow before you, I give my life to you.
I want my heart to be your throne in everything I do.

In God's time. I am learning God's time is perfect. It hasn't been an easy lesson for me to learn. As far back as I can remember, patience hasn't been something that has come very easily. Looking back at the many prayers God has answered, I have some hindsight. I see His wisdom and His love for me, not only in the fact that He hears me and attends to me, but that sometimes He waits. At first I didn't understand. I felt almost as if I were being teased. In my mind the wait didn't make sense. I wanted what I wanted in the least amount of time possible. I thought waiting was a bad thing, a harsh thing, but not anymore. I see waiting more and more as a loving thing. I am beginning to see my Heavenly Father as a good Father. He is a good parent. Hearing wait is still not easy, but as I grow to know Him more, I am learning it's always in love that He says that. I want my heart to be in a place of submission to Him. It's not because I am afraid of Him, but because I am learning to respect Him. He's teaching me trust in my very relationship with Him, because He is totally trustworthy. It hasn't been easy because I have spent a good part of my life trying to take care of me on my own. It wasn't because I was strong enough. It was because I was afraid. Jesus is proving my fears all wrong!

CAN YOU HEAR MY HEART CRY

Can you hear my heart cry? Who's going to be there for me?
When I wander home will the door be locked - will I have to use the key?

I'm not quite a woman, but I'm not a little girl; I'm somewhere in between.
How I need You so, though sometimes that's not the way it seems.

Someday, maybe I'll be your friend, but for now I must be your child.
If you don't teach me how to walk, how will I run life's miles.

Can you hear my heart cry? Who's going to be there for me?
When I wander home will the door be locked-will I have to use the key?

Sometimes I long for days gone by when you would rock me to sleep,
but that's not something you could know with this image must keep.

I want to make you proud of me, but I can't live your dreams.
I need your love to guide me, but still, you must set me free.

I'm not trying to prove you wrong. I just need you to understand,
I don't want to be a puppet with my strings in your hands.

Can you hear my heart cry? Who's going to be there for me?
When I wander home will the door be locked- will I have to use the key?

I'm not quite a woman, but I'm not a little girl-I'm somewhere in between,
and how I need you so though sometimes that's not the way it seems.

I'm in the middle of a journey that brings excitement and fear.
Sometimes you need to let, and sometimes to hold me near.

I'm not quite a woman, but I'm not a little girl-I'm somewhere in between
and how I need you so, though sometimes that's not the way it seems.

I remember those in between years so vividly. I wasn't a grown woman, but I wasn't exactly a child either. I just didn't know where I fit. Sometimes I wanted to just pull close to mom and dad and be their little girl again, but in my pride I wouldn't dare let them know. I thought I had an image to keep and I leaned on that rather than leaning on Jesus. I had so many secret fears, but I kept them hidden so well. I learned as I began to grow in Jesus that I didn't have any images to keep. I look at a lot of teenagers today and my heart aches. I see the emptiness and loneliness and searching in their eyes. I know they want someone older and stronger to lean on sometimes, or just hold them for a little while, but wouldn't dare admit it. I've seen young people close to me hurting so intensely because they seemingly had to take a back seat to their parent's lives. I wanted to reach out and fix it all for them, yet I knew the answer was the same for them as it was for me. Jesus. He is the one who will be there to answer the door. He is the one that can be a mother and father to children that so desperately need a mother or father. He is the one!

CAN YOU HEAR MY VOICE?

Can you hear my voice through the thunder of all your busy days?
Can you feel my heart beat when your heart wants to stray?

Will you let my love be enough when nothing else will satisfy?
Will you trust in My Son so you never have to die?

My ways may be different, you may not understand
but My ways are pure and simple-that's what love demands.

I'm not going to let you down, I've never failed before,
when I've filled your cup with life I'll fill it even more.

Can you hear My voice through the thunder of all your busy days?
Can you feel My heart beat when your heart wants to stray?

I love you as a mother tenderly loves her own.
You are flesh of My flesh and bone of My bones.

My ways may be different, you may not understand,
but My ways are pure and simple-that's what love demands.

DANIEL

What is he going to be like when he's three years old?
His life remains a mystery until the story unfolds.

Will he be short or tall, will his stature tell the tale?
What kind of man will he become when age removes the veil?

Will he choose the narrow road, the road Jesus walked upon?
Will he put his trust in Him, God's only perfect Son?

If someone points the way, if someone plants the seeds,
he can live in victory as God meets all his needs.

If his ears refuse to listen to this world's seductive lies,
he can be a free man with truth before his eyes.

Child, I pray the road you choose is the one Jesus walks upon,
I pray you will put your trust in Him, God's only perfect Son.

Then you'll know what it's like to be given wings,
as you soar in God's strength, you'll have the best of everything.

I met my nephew, Daniel, a few hours after he was born. That experience just reinforced what I already knew. There was a miracle right before my eyes. He was beautiful. His fingers and toes were perfect. Many prayers were answered. The birth was relatively easy, as far as giving birth goes. My sister came through just fine and now our family has a beautiful baby boy to love. I thought about what he would look like when he was older. Would his hair be blond or brown? What color would his eyes turn out to be? This was just curiosity. The more important question on my heart was what kind of man will he become? There are two roads from which to choose. My prayer for him will be that he chooses the road that Jesus walks. Life is not easy for any of us, but I think it is impossible without Jesus. My greatest desire for my nephew is that one day he will give his heart and his life to Jesus. I want the best for him. I know that is the best!

DID YOU SEE THE ROSES?

Did you see the roses in the garden? Did you see the beauty of them all?
Did you feel the touch of springtime, or hear its gentle call?

When the rain was finally over, did you smell the clean, moist air?
Did you know He shows us that His presence is everywhere?

God is like the rain that falls on desert land.
He is like the sun bringing light to every man.

Did you feel His mercy in your mother's soft, sweet touch?
It's just another way He shows He loves you very much.

When it seemed your heart was breaking, did you know He felt your pain?
Did you know His healing touch can make you whole again?

He is the generous giver of all good and perfect things.
Whatever humble hearts may need, that is what He brings.

Make a joyful noise unto God, all the earth; Sing forth the honor and glory of His name; make His praise glorious! Say to God, how awesome and fearfully glorious are Your works! Through the greatness of Your power shall Your enemies submit themselves to You.

Psalm 66:1,

DON'T RUN AWAY FROM GOD'S LOVE

I went into this city where life was meant to be,
instead I saw loneliness, fear and poverty.

I looked around and wondered why so many people did not hear
there's a King who has a table and it's very near.

There's provision for their hunger and provision for their thirst.
Healing for their sicknesses and deliverance from their hurt.

Don't run away from God's love, let Jesus lead you home.
There's a place for everyone, no one needs to be alone.

Looking back on my life I remembered hungry days,
when I longed for someone who would not go away.

Then Jesus showed me His banquet table and my food was the Life He gave,
when He died in my place, so I could be saved.

I walked around the city and it was so hard to understand,
so many hungry people refusing God's good hand.

Could it be they heard the words, but their hearts could not receive,
because they had hardened them and just refused to believe.

There's a King who has a table and it's very near.
The food is free to anyone who will choose to hear.

Don't run away from God's love, let Jesus lead you home.
There's a place for everyone, no one needs to be alone.

I spent a lot of time running away from God. When I finally stopped running from Him, I found what my heart had always been looking for. I had such a yearning to be known by someone who would understand who I was and be okay with that. I didn't realize for the first part of my life that God was the one who would satisfy all of my needs. Sin was a major factor in my life. As a teenager, I became rebellious and hardened. Still, the Lord held onto me. Even when I was doing wrong, I longed to be different. One day I decided I was going to stop running from God. I told Him I didn't want to walk alone anymore and I accepted His Son Jesus into my heart and received forgiveness for all of my sins. What He has shown me over the years is He is sufficient for all things. It is so hard for me to watch people struggle as I did, knowing that all they need to do is say yes, God, I am going to stop running.

FATHER

If your father on earth gave you bread when you were in need,
if your father on earth dried your tears when you skinned your knees,

How much more would your Father in heaven be willing to give-
the One who watches over you all the days you live?

He won't turn away or shun those who turn to Him.
How much more will He give to those who will let Him in?

He holds your tears in a bottle, He's counted each and every one,
and He will dry them all when the weeping's done.

God will make a way-there's nothing He can't do.
He will make a way because He cares for you.

If your father on earth gave you bread when you were in need,
if your father on earth dried your tears when you skinned your knees,

How much more would your Father in heaven be willing to give-
the One who watches over you all the days you live.

FATHER'S LOVE

The blessing came, it trickled down at first.
Not because I lacked value or intrinsic worth.

It came through His loving hands as He knew that I could bear.
The goodness He would give would be given to me with care.

I thought that I knew best-surely I needed it right now,
but His love would restrain Him even with tears upon my brow.

But Father don't you love me, don't you see the pain I'm in?
Couldn't you make it easier and calm the storm within?

Love is sometimes a mystery-it takes time to see its trace,
but it is there nonetheless though I cannot see His face.

The child part of me cannot seem to understand,
but it's only for a moment-soon I will see His hand.

Please forgive me for my impatience-Father I know that you know best.
Only in your strength can I ever come to perfect rest.

Though it's not your way, I strive and struggle again.
How I need your grace-even in giving in.

I waited patiently and expectantly for the Lord; and He inclined to me and heard my cry.

Psalm 40:1

FORGIVE

I heard the words they said to me, but I didn't want to hear.
Another arrow in a wounded heart was more than I could bear.

I ran to the meadow, I ran to the woods, somewhere to tend my wound.
I cried out to the one who knows, the one who can soothe.

Jesus, Jesus hear their words, it hurts to even know,
someone I once called friend could strike such a blow.

My child I can hear your cry, and I can feel it too.
Give to me your broken heart and I will make it new.

You told me to forgive them and let you take the pain
and shape me into someone who doesn't need to blame.

The blows the world will give you always leave a bruise,
but let me break and mold you into someone I can use.

At the cross I cried out too, but my words were Father forgive.
There I purchased life for you so that you could live.

Jesus, Jesus hear their words, it hurts to even know
someone I once called friend could strike such a blow.

My child I can hear your cry and I can feel it too.
Give your heart to me, and I will make it new.

There was a time in my life when I couldn't even imagine forgiving the people who hurt me. I mistakenly believed if I forgave them that I would be saying that what they did was okay. It wasn't until the Lord brought a Godly counselor into my life that I realized if I was ever going to be free I would have to forgive the people who hurt me so much. When harsh or critical words were spoken to me it felt like a burning arrow going into my heart. After the pain began to subside, then the shame would begin to creep in. Sometimes the humiliation I felt was so strong it was almost unbearable. In counseling I learned that I don't have to be a human punching bag for anyone's verbal abuse. I could stand up for myself in a Godly way. Sometimes that meant ending a relationship. In either case my job was to forgive-no matter what. The unforgivness (and there was plenty) in my heart was like spiritual cancer. The only way I could be free was to obey God's command to forgive. It was hard at first and sometimes I had to do it many times, but what began to happen was God started to soften my heart. What I learned was some of the people that hurt me the most were people that I loved the most. The Lord began to restore love in my heart for them and I even began to experience blessing from the very people I had harbored such a grudge against.

GOD'S LOVE

Yesterday was cold and wet though the sun was shining outside.
It was my heart that was dreary, it was me that wanted to hide.

I thought, will today be another day like so many days before?
Will I want to hide in my own world or along some lonely shore?

But then I saw the world around me change from summer into fall,
and all I could do was stand amazed and look at it in awe.

Lord your love for me is everywhere, you paint it in the Sky.
Please help me see the beauty is not to be passed by.

I thought about your love, and then my heart could see,
On dreary days it's there the same waiting just for me.

I see it in a mother's kiss when her child has fallen down,
I see it in a thousand ways-your beauty is all around.

Lord your love for me is everywhere, you paint it in the sky,
Please help me see the beauty is not to be passed by.

I think I understand now why flowers look the way they do,
In your love you gave these things so I would look to you.

I see it in a mother's kiss when her child has fallen down,
I see it in a thousand ways-your beauty is all around.

HE MIGHT TAKE YOU OUT OF THE FIRE

He might take you out of the fire, He might lead you through the flames,
but whichever way He may take you, His love remains the same.

He might take you down an easy path, or one with thorns here and there,
but whichever way He chooses He gives the grace to bear.

He carries you through seasons no matter what they may be,
though the rain may be blinding, and there's nothing you can see.

Having faith in His goodness and knowing His shoulders are strong is all that He requires,
as he leads you on quiet shores, or takes you through the fire.

There are no guarantees in life, but there's no question about His love.
It doesn't waver for a moment no matter what troubles may come.

Though He might take you out of the fire or lead you through the flames,
whichever way He may take you, His love remains the same.

I don't like trials, especially big ones. Every time He brings me through something a little rough. I think "I sure am glad that's over, I hope this is the last one". So far, it hasn't been. I guess when I cross to the other side, that's when I can be sure that there will be no more trials. Sometimes I struggle with not understanding. I feel, if He would just let me in on what He's doing, I could handle it a lot better. A big part of letting God be God, I'm learning is that it's okay when He doesn't let me in on it. It doesn't mean He doesn't care. It just means He really knows what He is doing. I guess, sometimes I feel as if it is adding insult to injury when He won't even tell me why when I have to endure the trial in the first place. What He has been trying to drive home to me is that He loves me in spite of anything that happens, or anything He allows. None of this affects His love. That is never in question, though sometimes in my mind it is. My prayer today Has been, "Lord help me to trust you even when it's hard, and I don't understand". I think I am coming to the place where I realize He has to give me that kind of trust.

ALABASTER JAR

Let the alabaster jar be broken, let the oil run through.
Let the Lord touch your heart and do what He wants to do.

His blessings will flow through you to those that are in need.
Let the jar be broken so His Spirit can flow free.

Holding on to dreams may seem the thing to do,
but until you hand them over, the oil can't run through.

Security comes in trusting that God's heart is very good,
not in trusting idols made of metal, stone, or wood.

We are His workmanship, the clay within His hands.
He longs to call us children; He longs to call us friends.

Let the alabaster jar be broken, let the oil run through.
Let the Lord touch your heart and do what He wants to do.

Holding on to dreams may seem the thing to do,
but until you hand them over, the oil can't run through.

When Mary broke the alabaster jar and let the spikenard run over Jesus, she was giving the very best she had to give. Her offering was pure and complete. There was nothing lacking because she gave Him the best. That's what He wants from our lives. When we accept Jesus into our hearts, our bodies become the temples of God's Holy Spirit. He wants to make us into vessels for His use. Our lives are like alabaster jars to Him. When we surrender all we have and are — our hearts, bodies, ambitions, relationships, and finances — then He can truly flow through us. Surrendering to Him doesn't mean that we have to give up abundant life. On the contrary, when we surrender, we enter into the most abundant life possible. Let the alabaster jars of our lives be broken, so His Spirit can flow through us and bring others to Him.

LULLABY

When I was a little girl my mom would sing me songs.
When I was afraid she'd sing-suddenly I felt strong.

Sometimes the wind would blow, it seemed angry and fierce to me,
but in my mother's arms the fear just had to flee.

Jesus, you remind me of a lullaby, soft and kind and good.
When I was afraid you gently understood.

Like a mother who calms her child, you calm the storm within.
You remind me of a lullaby, you are the Master of the wind.

I know no fear will ever rule-my heart is quiet and still.
In your love you hold me-I'm resting in your will.

When I was a little girl, my mom would sing me songs.
When I was afraid she'd sing-suddenly I felt strong.

Sometimes the wind would blow, it seemed angry and fierce to me,
but in my mother's arms the fear just had to flee.

Jesus, you remind me of a lullaby, soft and kind and good.
When I was afraid, you gently understood.

Like a mother who calms her child, you calm the storm within.
You remind me of a lullaby, you are the Master of the wind.

JESUS

Jesus, Jesus, I want to be like you.
Jesus, Jesus, show me what to do.

I bow before you. I submit to do Your will.
Help me take the mountains and turn them into hills.

I want to be a humble child. I want to know Your ways.
I will give You all of me; teach me to obey.

I know Your hand is gentle. I trust that You know best.
My heart is longing just for You. You give me perfect rest.

Jesus, Jesus, I want to be like you.
Jesus, Jesus, show me what to do.

I want to serve You faithfully; keep me from all wrong.
You fill my heart with melody. My life will be Your song.

Every path that I take is directed by Your steps.
My heart is longing just for You. You give me perfect rest.

Jesus, Jesus, I want to be like You.
Jesus, Jesus, show me what to do.

*Take My yoke upon you and learn of Me, for I am gentle
(meek) and humble (lowly) in heart, and you will find rest
(relief and ease and refreshment and recreation and blessed
quite) for your souls.*

Matthew 11:29

IT'S A LOVE SONG

It's a love song in the middle of the night that I sing to you,
a song of longing to be by your side where everything is new.

My heart is like a deep well-waiting to be filled.
Only you can satisfy, I know that is your will.

All around me there have been casualties in a war not meant to be,
but I heard you speaking softly, find a place in me.

It's a love song in the middle of the night that I sing to you,
a song of longing to be by your side where everything is new.

My name is written in your book, I accepted your gift of grace,
salvation is the answer for those who will win the race.

Now, fear is just a shadow, and your love will cast it down.
You are my only refuge, I am no longer bound.

It's a love song in the middle of the night that I sing to you,
a song of longing to be by your side where everything is new.

LIKE AN ORDINARY STONE

Like an ordinary stone with no beauty to be seen;
I was tossed upon the ground and trampled by men's feet.

I didn't know the love of God though it was always there;
He loved me when I longed for love with tender loving care.

I will always praise you, Lord, for taking me as your own;
when I was tossed upon the ground like an ordinary stone.

Some men may shine like diamonds, on the outside the glitter shows,
but if they don't know Jesus glitter is all they know.

His eyes are forever upon me, he never turns away
and He showers me with mercy as I walk through all my days.

Like an ordinary stone with no beauty to be seen;
I was tossed upon the ground and trampled by men's feet.

I didn't know the love of God though he was always there;
He loved me when I longed for love with tender loving care.

I will always praise you, Lord, for taking me as your own,
when I was tossed upon the ground like an ordinary stone.

When I was in junior high school, that's how I felt about myself most of the time-like I was an ordinary stone with no beauty to be seen. My sense of worth was mostly on the negative side. I was filled with self-doubt and hatred. I felt like I was anything but beautiful. I didn't know Jesus when I was in school. I didn't accept Him until I was in my early twenties. Still, I couldn't begin to grasp my worth or importance to Him. One evening I was spending some quiet time in my room . I was just pouring my heart out to Him. That's when I heard it. "You're precious to me." I know it was the Lord, because I could never have come up with something like that on my own. I didn't hear it audibly with my ears, but I heard it in my mind. I knew beyond a doubt that Jesus was saying something very important to me and He meant it. That was a major turning point. I took Him at His word, and for the first time in my life I began to see myself as something other than an ordinary stone. It wasn't that I wasn't always precious to Him, even when I was far away in sin, it was that I couldn't hear it until that moment. What a wonderful blessing and revelation!

THANK YOU FOR LOVING ME THAT MUCH

When the path that I chose was leading to troubles unseen Your mighty hand was there.
I didn't know it then but you showed how much You care.

Sometimes You allowed me to stumble even to feel the pain,
hoping I wouldn't choose to go down that path again.

Thank you for loving me that much, thank you for standing in my way,
when I thought I knew where I was going, but there was a price to pay.

Your loving eyes kept watching me, your gentle hand would guide,
until I changed my mind and laid down my foolish pride.

Even when I didn't understand and was blinded by my tears,
You silently kept on holding me to comfort all my fears.

As a child I saw things my way, choosing to go where feelings would lead
never knowing where I would end up or how far from You I'd be.

Sometimes You let me fall down, but always to get back up again,
in Your love you even led me when I wouldn't let You in.

Thank you for loving me that much, thank you for standing in my way,
when I thought I knew where I was going, but there was a price to pay.

I like to use the example of poison ivy a lot. I tell people that if you don't want to get poison ivy, don't sit in the poison ivy patch. That is what sin is like. Before I came to the Lord, I did plenty of sitting in poison ivy. I used to think that when I got caught, or someone held me accountable, it was my misfortune at having gotten caught. The Lord is teaching me to look at the bigger picture, however. The ultimate consequence of sin is death and had I remained in my sin it would have caught up with me, eventually. Now, I thank the Lord for the people he put in my path to hold me accountable and even for the times I "got caught". Life is a lot more simple and enjoyable when I stay out of the poison ivy patch!

MOTHER'S POEM

It's not an ending but a beginning, another bridge to cross,
not a forever goodbye or a son that is lost.

It is a flower blooming, becoming what it was meant to be;
a boy now a man, an eagle just set free.

The distance can be painful but love will endure,
until that season's over and the soldier returns for sure.

You say goodbye to your firstborn, but then hello to your friend,
though another chapter closes, the story doesn't end.

One day you'll walk side by side and you'll see the man he's become,
the soldier for a little while…forever your son.

I've had the pleasure and the immense joy of watching my niece and nephews grow up. Although I have no children of my own, I have been richly blessed to be a part of my sister and brothers children's lives. When my oldest nephew made the decision to go into the army it was a very difficult time for my sister. Not only was her first born leaving the nest, he was joining the military at a very unstable time. I think she is learning more than ever that the only safe place for her children is in God's care. She can't be there with him. She can't protect him from things the way she could when he was a child. She can't, but God can and He will. What is so comforting is that His love for us-His children- is so great it can't begin to be measured. He had to let go of His Son, Jesus, because there was a much bigger purpose. Sometimes love means letting go as much as it means holding on. I know that one day my nephew will return from his tour in the army and my sister will have gained a friend.

THE FACE IN THE MIRROR

The face in the mirror has changed today. I finally learned to see.
I don't have to be someone else. It's fine just being me.

I used to see the flaws I had. I tried to turn away,
but Jesus helped me see the truth, and the face in the mirror has changed today.

In Your image, Lord, You crafted me. I bear Your Holy touch.
In Your love You gave me life. You gave so very much.

I saw, before, a picture never meant to have a frame;
a face with no identity, a person with no name.

I tried to change God's perfect plan and became who I was not
until He opened up my eyes and then I saw my lot.

In Your image, Lord, you crafted me. I bear Your Holy touch.
In Your love You gave me life. You gave so very much.

I'm not a lonely wanderer now, nor a person with no name.
I don't see a worthless picture never meant to have a frame.

The face in the mirror has changed today. I finally learned to see
I don't have to be someone else. It's fine just being me.

In Your image, Lord, You crafted me. I bear Your Holy touch.
In Your love You gave me life. You gave so very much.

*God said, Let us make mankind in Our image, after Our likeness, and let them have
complete authority over the fish of the sea, the birds of the air, the beasts, and over all of the
earth, and over everything that creeps upon the earth.*

Genesis 1:26

PRAISE

I rise in the morning to praise you, Lord.
I always see before me the beauty of your world.

My heart is filled with gratitude for each new day that you give,
and I'll rise in the morning to praise you Lord, as long as I live.

You wake me with your gentle touch with a kiss of sunlight on my face,
and you hold me close to you with your strong embrace.

Nighttime may bring closure to the day that came and went,
but tomorrow I will praise you until that day is spent.

You surround me with your loveliness, it's forever before my eyes,
from the flowers in my garden to the stars up in the sky.

I rise in the morning to praise you, Lord.
I always see before me the beauty of your world.

My heart is filled with gratitude for each new day that you give,
and I'll rise in the morning to praise you Lord, as long as I live.

NOT BY MIGHT, NOR BY POWER

I can do all things through Christ who strengthens me,
whether I have to face a giant or learn to rest beneath a tree.

I don't have to worry about anything, that's God's gentle command,
though I am a warrior, Jesus takes the land.

Not by might nor by power but by His Spirit says the Lord,
It's written for eternity, written in His Word.

There's nothing He can't do through me if I lay my whole life down.
I'll find in Him humility and a heart and mind that's sound.

Though I am a warrior, Jesus takes the land.
I don't have to worry about anything, that's God's gentle command.

In the darkness of the night when I want to tremble inside,
Jesus is my anchor, He's right there by my side.

Not by might nor by power but by His Spirit says the Lord,
it's written for eternity, written in His Word.

If I were in miry clay with enemies everywhere,
if I put my trust in Him, He would be right there.

He is a mighty deliverer, and He knows me by my name,
Jesus is the conqueror of all my guilt and shame.

Not by might nor by power but by His Spirit says the Lord,
it's written for eternity, written in His Word.

I recently was laid off from my job. While I am enjoying my time off I know eventually I will have to go back to work. My biggest challenge is trusting God to provide. It's not that I think He won't, because He has time and time again, it's just that there is a part of me that wants to be in control. I don't completely understand it because I know He is good. I choose to trust, but inside the battle goes on. There is something I can't quite put my finger on that wants me to strive in my own strength, to worry and to struggle until I am worn out. That is not God's way. The Bible says Not by Might nor by Power, but by My Spirit says the Lord. It's not just a nice saying. I know if I want to live my life in peace and be free from strife and worry, I have to take this seriously. God really means it. I'm not saying that I can just sit around and wait for Him to drop it in my lap, but if I am doing everything I can, then worry has no place. He is infinitely good and infinitely faithful. I choose to trust Him with my life! The clincher is, I can't even in my own strength not worry, struggle and strive. Only in Him can I find the strength to obey. When I choose to obey, that frees Him up to do the work that He needs to do.

THE SUN WILL RISE AGAIN

The sun will rise tomorrow just like it always does.
The darkness of the night will pass, and all will be as it was.

Peace will begin to flow again, and the pain you feel will pass.
The darkness will be just a memory, and rest will come at last.

The flowers will bloom again in April, after the long winter flees away
and hope will rise within you as you begin another day.

Joy will find a place to rest deep within your heart,
with no reason left to shed your tears, you have a brand new start.

I've never seen a thunder storm that doesn't have an end.
I've never seen a calm heart that's not greater than the wind.

Trials come and trials go tempered by God's hand.
He is the foundation in spite of shifting sand.

The sun will rise tomorrow just like it always does.
The darkness of the night will pass and all will be as it was.

Weeping may endure for a night, but joy comes in the morning.
Psalm 30:5

NEW MERCIES

I See your new mercies every day,
from the sun that faithfully rises to the stars that light the way.

My eyes can see your majesty every time I turn around.
My ears can hear your music in the rushing water's sound.

Blessed am I to be your child, all your goodness you impart to me.
What wonderful things I have seen because you have helped me see.

I won't take for granted your good heart anymore,
because I see your loveliness through an open door.

Every day I see new miracles that you choose to let me see,
and I know that it's a reflection of the love you feel for me.

I see your new mercies every day,
from the sun that faithfully rises to the stars that light the way.

My eyes can see your majesty every time I turn around.
My ears can hear your music in the rushing water's sound.

Blessed am I to be your child, all your goodness you impart to me.
What wonderful things I have seen because you have helped me see.

The Bible says that we can see God's glory in His creation. I have
seen sunsets that take my breath away. I have seen water that shines
like diamonds on a bright summer day as the sun causes a jewel like
sparkle. I have watched deer sprint from field to field as I have
enjoyed an evening walk. I realized one day that I was seeing God's
glory right before my eyes. His handiwork is everywhere. The only
way I can't see is if I walk through life with my eyes closed. In His
love for me these are just a few of His wonderful gifts. I can see His
new mercies every day.

RAINBOW

I know there's going to be a rainbow after every storm,
a promise given for the hard times, when it seems hard to endure.

My life is in my Father's hands no matter what the skies may do.
Tomorrow will bring the sunshine when the storm is through.

I can rest assured Jesus will not let go.
When the weather is foreboding-when storm clouds are hanging low.

Even if my friends should leave, and my family can't understand,
I am not alone because I'm resting in His hands.

I know there's going to be a rainbow after every storm,
a promise given for the hard times, when it seems hard to endure.

I will lift up my eyes to the hills from whence shall my help come? My help comes from the Lord, who made heaven and earth. He will not allow your foot to slip or to be moved; He who keeps you will not slumber.

Psalm 121:1,3

NEW LIFE

Who would take a withered rose and make it something new,
rising in the morning to greet the morning dew.

Who would want to look at something with no shine,
and turn it into hope, leaving the grayness behind.

You took me Lord as I was and told me what I could be,
if I gave my heart to you, you'd give me eyes to see.

I used to run from mirrors, because I thought they could not lie,
and what I saw I didn't like, so I just passed them by.

One day I dared to look beyond reflections in the glass
and heard a voice say to me, I'll change you if you ask.

He said "I see all of you and all that you can be,
and that is not a wilted rose striving to be free".

At first I was afraid, because His love seemed far away
but as I grew to know Him, I wanted Him to stay.

You took me Lord as I was and told me what I could be.
If I gave my heart to you, you'd give me eyes to see.

O Lord, the God of my salvation, I have cried to You for help
by day; at night I am in your presence. Let my prayer come
before You and really enter into Your presence; incline Your
ear to my cry!

Psalm 88 1,2

MOUNTAIN I DON'T HAVE TO BE AFRAID OF YOU!

Mountain I don't have to be afraid of you,
because my Lord is going to bring me through.

I'm going to soar over you like an eagle just set free.
I've got the Holy Spirit living inside of me.

Mercy goes before me, and I'm surrounded by God's grace.
I'm running with conviction, and I'm going to win the race.

The lion roars, the tiger growls, but my heart will not be moved.
My shelter is the Lord Himself-my heart will not be moved.

Mountain I don't have to be afraid of you,
Because my Lord is going to bring me through.

I'm going to soar over you like an eagle just set free.
I've got the Holy Spirit living inside of me.

WHO IS STRONGER?

What happens when the world gives way right beneath your feet
and the only thing that now seems sure is destruction and defeat?

The enemy is larger than shadows in the night
lurking everywhere and urging you to fight.

Who is stronger, the one who knocks you down, or the one who picks you up,
the one who pours the wrath or the one who holds the cup?

Jesus, with His tender heart will gently bring you through,
when the world gives way beneath your feet and there's nothing left to do.

He will lift you higher than all the pain you've ever known
and put you back on solid ground with Him upon the throne.

Who is stronger, the one who knocks you down or the one who picks you up,
the one who pours the wrath or the one who holds the cup?

I think life is like that sometimes. You just get knocked off of your feet.
Sometimes it's just one of those things that happen as a result of living in a
fallen world and sometimes it is a carefully planned attack from satan,
himself. Either way, it's no fun having the breath knocked out of you. When I
was growing up I spent a lot of my time riding horses. My grandfather told
me that if the horse throws you off you have get right back on. I guess I look
at life that way, sometimes. We all are going to get knocked down, now and
then. The one who makes the difference between staying down and getting
back up is Jesus. He's there always to lift up and heal and encourage. Being
willing to get up is a big part of the battle. Satan can strike a fierce blow, but
with God he's the loser every time!

THERE'S A SEASON

There's a season for the rains to come and a season for them to cease.
There's a season for our trials and a season for our peace.

Some things are for a lifetime, some things will endure
but all these things to build our faith into one that is pure.

There are hills to climb, but with Jesus, not alone.
He's the one who will lead all His sheep back home.

Tomorrow may be different from what yesterday has been
but there is no fear in changes when our trust is in Him.

The things that might defeat me can serve to make me strong
and when they have passed by I see He's been there all along.

There's a season for the rains to come and a season for them to cease.
There's a season for our trials and a season for our peace.

Some things are for a lifetime, some things will endure
but all these things to build our faith into one that is pure.

*To everything there is a season, and a time for every matter or
purpose under heaven.*

Ecclesiastics 3:1

VICTORY IN MY HEART

I feel victory in my heart from a battle that's hard won.
I know it's coming soon: Satan will be undone.

I feel the hope of life again moving in my soul.
I know I have the victory and soon will be made whole.

Jesus is filled with love, but He's a warrior too.
He holds the battle in His hands, to give life back to you.

There's no such thing as failure if I never quit the race.
I can win only if I learn to accept His grace.

There's grace to save and grace to hold. I know just where I stand.
I will be the winner if the victory is from His hands.

Jesus is filled with love, but He's a warrior too.
He holds the battle in His hands to give life back to you.

I feel the hope of life again moving in my soul.
I will have the victory, and soon will be made whole.

I feel it in my heart from a battle that's hard won.
I know it's coming soon - Satan will be undone.

Jesus is filled with love, but He's a warrior too.
He holds the battle in His hands to give life back to you.

*And all this assembly shall know that the Lord saves not with sword
and spear; for the battle is the Lord's, and He will give you into our
hands.*

I Samuel 17:47

MY FATHER KNOWS

My Father knows what's around each bend.
He knows how much sunshine and how much rain to give.

The boundaries of the oceans rest within His hands.
It cannot cross its limits to overtake the land.

His ways are always perfect, and His heart is always right.
His desire is for His children who are precious in His sight.

The hurting find a refuge, the homeless find a home.
The ones who fear can be at peace and the lonely-no more alone.

In His love He created me, and in His love He redeems-
in His love He created, and in His love He redeems.

Bridges are built and walls come down as He sets free those bound by hate,
and prayers are always answered for those who find the time to wait.

His ways are always perfect, and His heart is always right.
His desire is for His children who are precious in His sight.

I remember when I was a little girl, sometimes my dad would pick me up and put me on his shoulders. I felt like I was literally on top of the world. It seemed as if nothing could ever hurt me. My dad was so strong. I know my dad would have protected me from all of the hurts that life deals out if he could have. In my mind, as a child, what I didn't realize was that my dad too, was human. I guess I thought he could do anything. I went through a period in my life where I felt betrayed and angry at him for the times he wasn't able to protect me. My expectations of him were too great, and there was no room for understanding. Then I met Jesus. I found He was able to protect me and He was big enough for my expectations. He is perfect as His Father is perfect. Because of Jesus, I have the privilege of being able to call His Father my Father, too. He tore down the walls and built the bridge, so I could come home to my Heavenly Father's arms where I truly belong. As I grew in my walk with the Lord, I was able to put things into a better perspective. I could accept that my dad truly loved me, but He was not God. His shoulders were strong, but only God's shoulders are strong enough for all of my cares. In that acceptance, I was also able to forgive. Now, I look at my dad and can truly appreciate him and see what a blessing that he has been and is in my life.

Thank you Jesus for my earthly father!

THE BLESSING

I was looking for a blessing from my father's hand,
but he couldn't seem to hear my cry. He didn't understand.

I walked through my childhood waiting for the day
I'd see him look at who I was, and his smile would come my way.

I yearned for his approval the way a daughter does.
I couldn't accept the distance; I was looking for his love.

"Father will You bless me, make my world all right?
Will you take this hurt away that I live with day and night?"

One day I heard an answer, but my earthly father didn't reply.
It was my Father in heaven who heard my painful cry.

"Yes, I will bless you. Take my hand and you will see
all the things I've planned for you, if you'll come with Me."

I learned I wasn't destined to forever be without,
even if I wondered and it sometimes turned to doubt.

My dad was not a bad man. He just had no blessing to give;
it wasn't passed on down to him. It was time to just forgive.

"Father will You bless me, make my world all right?
Will You take this hurt away that I live with day and night?"

I found hope through God's love. He blessed me with Himself.
I'm not a victim of poverty, but a bearer of His wealth.

I love my dad with all of my heart. For a long time, though, I had
my doubts about how he felt about me. He couldn't seem to express
his feelings toward me. That is just not my dad's way. I can see that
now, but growing up, I felt as if I were always disappointing him. I
believed if I could just live up to some invisible expectation,
everything would be fine. The problem was I could never live up to
this. My heart was aching and yearning for acceptance and approval
and love, but the only way I thought I could get it was to earn it.
When I came to Jesus, however, it wasn't that way. He said I love
you freely. You don't have to earn it. He said I was precious to Him.
It was like a spring shower in a desert that hadn't known rain in a
long, long time. I did receive the blessing-from my Heavenly Father!
I also was able to give up expectations that I carried for my earthly
dad. I was able to see how many blessings I did receive from him.

NEW MORNING

Last night my room was dark with shadows everywhere.
The curtains hid the moonlight, but there was no despair.

I know I'm held by Jesus in daytime or in night
and even where there's shadows I can still see by His light.

Now there's a new morning just like my life is new
and satan is the loser because Jesus brought me through.

At first I was afraid and my mind just wouldn't rest
but God is always faithful and He knows what is best.

Sometimes it takes the darkness and trials everywhere
to see there is no better place than resting in His care.

There will be a new morning just like my life is new,
and satan will be the loser because Jesus brings me through.

I've seen so many shadows cast by evils lie
but I've learned my Lord is faithful and always hears my cry.

Now there's a new morning just like my life is new
and satan is the loser because Jesus brought me through.

*He who dwells in the secret place of the Most High shall remain
stable and fixed under the shadow of the Almighty*

Psalm 91:1

RUNAWAY CHILDREN

Runaway children please come home, your Father is calling you.
He will forgive you, Jesus is kind, He'll show you what to do.

Each on of us is a prodigal, each one of us has run away
but Father is still calling and waiting every day.

There's a hell to turn away from and only heaven to gain
a devil to be defeated and healing from all pain.

A mile is too far to go from God's loving arms
but ten thousand aren't too far if we want shelter from the storm.

Runaway children please come home, your Father is calling you.
He will forgive you, Jesus is kind, He'll show you what to do.

Each one of us is a prodigal, each one of us has run away
but Father is still calling and waiting every day.

There's a hell to turn away from and only heaven to gain
a devil to be defeated and healing from all pain.

A mile is too far to go from God's loving arms
but ten thousand aren't too far if we want shelter from the storm.

Runaway children please come home your Father is calling you.
He will forgive you, Jesus is kind, He'll show you what to do.

*For God so greatly loved and dearly prized the world that He
gave up His only begotten Son, so that whoever believes in Him
shall not perish but have eternal life.*
John 3:16

WHO'SE GOING TO PICK UP THE PIECES?

Who's going to pick up the pieces of a broken heart when that heart is only four?
Who's going to teach a child love when they live behind locked doors?

Walls come in many forms-sometimes inside there the highest of them all,
but who's going to pick up the pieces when no one is around when she calls?

I know you died for children, Lord-you carried all that pain.
You can stop the hurting, you didn't die in vain.

I know you live for me today, you're higher than the walls.
You're picking up the pieces-you heard me when I called.

It only takes a few harsh words and a child can believe,
they're to blame for everything-even for their needs.

Who's going to pick up the pieces of a broken heart when that heart is only four?
Who's going to teach a child love when they live behind locked doors?

I know you died for children Lord-you carried all that pain.
You can stop the hurting, you didn't die in vain.

When I was a little girl, I remember being so sensitive. I was always getting my feelings hurt, but I don't believe that many people knew that, because on the outside I put up a false façade. Even at such a young age, I knew how to erect walls. One time after being hurt I went upstairs to my room to be alone. The shame on top of the hurt was almost more than I could bear. I sat on the floor and hung my head in humiliation. All of the sudden I felt something lift my heart. It was as if Jesus just reached inside and took it all away. I didn't know that at the time, but looking back I realized that He knew I couldn't bear the pain, so He just took it away. What a loving, good Heavenly Father. I didn't know enough at that time to reach out to Him, but it didn't matter. He reached out to me in my need. Thank you Jesus!

ABOUT THE AUTHOR

She has written Christian & Inspirational poetry for over twenty years. Her desire is to express the love and faithfulness of Jesus Christ.

Printed in the United States
By Bookmasters